THE
YOUNG LAD
WHO LOST HIS
NIGHTSHIRT

William B. Caldwell, B.S., M.Div.

WESTBOW
P R E S S®
A DIVISION OF THOMAS NELSON
& ZONDERVAN

WestBow Press books may be ordered through booksellers or by contacting:

WestBow Press
A Division of Thomas Nelson & Zondervan
1663 Liberty Drive
Bloomington, IN 47403
www.westbowpress.com
1 (866) 928-1240

Interior Image Credit: Marilyn Frank

ISBN: 978-1-9736-7156-5 (sc)
ISBN: 978-1-9736-7157-2 (hc)
ISBN: 978-1-9736-7155-8 (e)

Library of Congress Control Number: 2019911378

Print information available on the last page.

WestBow Press rev. date: 08/05/2019

INTRODUCTION

Over the many years in ministry, I have been giving brief "children's sermons" as an addition to the main order of worship. The topics and "characters" were Biblically based, using the Old and New Testaments.

As noted earlier, I traveled many times to the Holy Land, and the Bible came alive to me then; the visual memories became embedded in my mind, heart, and soul.

From these eye-opening experiences, there came a tugging on my soul to share stories of a young person's first-hand experience as it most likely would have occurred.

The young man herein was from a Jewish family, steeped in rituals and customs. His family and he became great friends with Jesus and ultimately played an integral part in the last days of Jesus. This lad's story permeates the second book of the New Testament.

ACKNOWLEDGEMENTS

W hen I began to take on the writing of this book, I thought of the many children who sat at my feet in the churches where I served as pastor. It was those times that I gave a children's sermon. Many thanks to those now adults, who were respectful, listened, and were open to The Word. My appreciation goes to their parents as well. Those parents encouraged me over the years to write. Today, I am 88 years old, and herein is my first attempt.

Individually, the following persons were my unique and special supporters, whom I deeply appreciate:

Karen Salanda, who typed the entire project where needed.

Marsha Looysen critiqued the content, offered constructive ideas, and did all the proof-reading.

Marilyn Frank has created our illustrations with her inimitable talent and suggestions.

Matt Phillips has technologically gathered all the parts and constructed the completed original document.

Dr. James Fleming, my friend and my professor in Israel, whose wisdom and knowledge has touched me immeasurably.

To each of you, I say, "Thank you" very much.

That having been said, I want to personally mention my very beloved wife of 58 years, Julie. She has stood by me throughout this whole project with gigantic patience, grace, and fortitude. Thank you, honey, I could not have done this without your support.

THE YOUNG LAD WHO LOST HIS NIGHT SHIRT

"**A** story about a night shirt?" you may ask. And to that, I would reply, "Yes", but before we get to that night, there are some things I need to tell you in order to help you picture the results.

My name is John Mark. My family's home in Jerusalem has a furnished room above our sleeping quarters, and that room is reached by the outside staircase. When you enter this upper room, you will find in the center a table that is U-shaped. The center of this table is where the servant may serve the meal. Around the outside of this table are cushions, and those eating this meal will lie down on their left side and use their right hand to eat the meal.

In one corner of this special room there is a cabinet where we keep table lamps, oil for the lamps, and extra dishes.

Next to the door is a table called the hospitality table. It has a flask of sweet oil, a pitcher for water, a washbasin and a towel.

Usually, our upper room is in great demand during the season of Passover. But it has not been rented yet, and Passover is only a few days away.

Mother regularly goes down to the Pool of Siloam and fills up a water jug and brings it back to our house. However, today she asked Father to go to the pool and fill a water jug. She also suggested that Father take me, John Mark, to go along with him and bring an extra pot of water back from the pool. When we reached the pool, we found a long line of women waiting to fill their pots; we stood in line and waited our turn. Soon we were able to go down the steps and fill our jugs.

When we were going back up to our home, I noticed that there were two men following us. I told Father what I had seen, and he nodded his head that he, too, had seen the two men. When we entered the courtyard, the two men entered right behind us. They approached my mother, who was waiting for us in the courtyard. Father went to empty his jug into the stone water pot that was there in the courtyard, while I went upstairs and into the furnished upper room to fill the water pot there.

When I came out of the upper room, I saw that the two men who followed us home were gone.

I went down the steps, and Mother came over with a big smile on her face. She said, "Jesus and his disciples are going to use our furnished upper room to celebrate the Passover meal."

Father led Mother and me up the stairs and into the upper room. We all had to prepare that room for the celebration. When the meal is served, Jesus will be the host, and His chosen disciples will be seated as to their rank of importance around the table. Father led us in a prayer saying, "Blessed art thou, O Lord our God, King of the universe, who has sanctified us by the commandments to remove the leaven from this room." (Ancient Hebrew Prayer)

I was now put in charge of cleaning the upper room to make sure that all pieces of food might be removed. First, I removed the cushions from around the table and took them outside; here I beat and shook them to remove any crumbs that might have been left on them. I then placed them over the sides of the roof to dry in the sun.

Entering the room, I took a towel from the cabinet and dipped it in the water in the basin. I then began to wipe the table down to remove any crumbs that might be still on the table. Now it was time to sweep the floor. I began in the corners of the room and began to sweep. Then, I continued sweeping around the floor next to the table, cabinet, and the stone water pots on the table of hospitality. Once I had all the crumbs in one pile, I swept them out the door and let the wind blow them away. I could now replace the cushions and set the table with plates, bowls and glasses from the storage cabinet.

Now, I called Father and Mother to come up and inspect the room. They were to make sure that there were no crumbs in the room and that it was clean. Mother took a small lamp that father had lit, and she began to go around to each of the corners of the room. She held the lamp down close to the corners to make sure with this light that there were no crumbs there. Then she inspected the table, looking at the plates, bowls, and glasses. She found that some of the plates were cracked, and some of the wine glasses were chipped, so she decided that we should replace the tableware with new plates, bowls, and wine glasses.

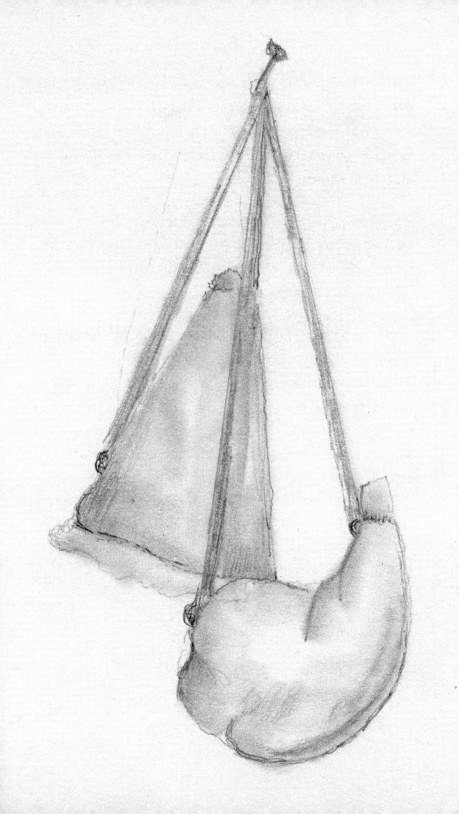

These two wine skins are unique in and of themselves; one is old and one is new. The use of the older wrinkled one was only for water. The newer one was used in the making of new wines from fresh grape juice and was then placed in goat skins and allowed to ferment.

Then, she prepared a shopping list for each of us to use when we went shopping. Father's list was to go to the Sheep Gate; here lambs were sold and bought and then taken into the temple courtyard, where the lambs were sacrificed.

Father bought a young lamb and took it into the courtyard to be sacrificed. Father also needed to go to a shop in the market where he was to buy a large copper pot. The final stop he needed to make was to go to a shop to buy wine. The wine's container was made of goatskin. Father bought two skins of wine and then returned home with all that he purchased.

Mother's shopping list consisted of the following items: potatoes, carrots, garlic, honey, olives, dates, raisins, radishes, onions, eggs, celery, walnuts, cucumbers, parsley, lentils, cinnamon sticks, cloves, apricots, figs, and nuts.

In those days, in spite of no refrigeration, there was an abundance of fresh vegetables and fresh fruit. The environment was conducive to the growing and cultivation nearly year round.

The markets were a delightful place for the women to meet and engage in the news of the day and stories of their families' lives.

When Mother and Father had decided to replace the old cracked and chipped dishes and wine glasses, it then became my job to shop for the replacements. I took a large basket and headed to the shops in the market that sold plates, bowls, and wine glasses.

I love to go to Jerusalem markets where many of my friends' families own little shops. Gathering in the large plaza's entrance is always where my friends and I have fun. It is there where we can play games, sing, and dance. However, today is not a day when that will happen. I had too much shopping to do in preparation for the Passover celebration meal that Jesus and his disciples would share in the upper room in my house.

Today is the day of preparation for Passover. It is the day before the week when Passover begins, and my mother has need of some more items for the meal she is preparing for us. She has made a list, and I am on the way first to the Spice Shop.

It was amazing how many people were out shopping. I found myself in the back of a large crowd, and from a distance, I saw my friend, Sara, who was serving another customer. Her parents owned the shop, and Sara was so much fun as a friend. She mouthed the words to me, "I will be with you in a minute." It was not long before she began to weave her way toward where I was standing. She said, "Hi, Mark! What do you need?"

I answered, "I need quite a few things for our Passover meal, and first of all I need some Dead Sea salt, garlic, and a bundle of parsley."

Her response was quick with, "I will get them and be right back." She left and returned quickly carrying a basketful of items Mother needed. There were several lumps of salt; the lumps were not all pure, so I picked through them and chose the ones I thought Mother would prefer. After placing the salt in my basket, I reached for the garlic bulbs; some were soft and mushy, but several were just perfect – so into the basket. The bundles of parsley she brought were fresh and a lush, bright green. They were added quickly to the other items.

"How much?" I asked Sara.

"Six small copper coins," she replied.

I countered with, "Four copper coins!"

This is a form of bargaining called "haggling". Haggling is quite well accepted in this part of the world. We settled for three small coins, and I was off to my next destination.

My next stop was at the Potter's Shop; Mother realized we needed new tableware. As I entered the Potter's Shop, I saw that he was busy turning the potter's wheel with a big glob of clay on the top wheel.

Making pottery is a very precise activity, and one needs to be very careful. As the potter used his foot on the floor where a piece of equipment was used to turn the wheels necessary to complete the task, he explained, "I am starting to create a bowl and will be right with you."

During this time in history, the people who would be participating in the Passover meal would purchase gifts for family and friends. Often the gifts were pottery objects unique to the purchase of these pieces of pottery was that Jerusalem was the only city where these objects would be available.

I stood fascinated, as I saw a bowl start to take shape from the lump of clay.

Once he completed the task, he asked, "What do you need?"

I responded, "My Mother needs new mid-sized tableware."

"James", the potter called to his son.

James set down two bowls he carried and asked, "What can I help you with?"

Once I responded with what was needed, he disappeared back to the room where the tableware was stored. Soon James returned with items for me to inspect and make my choices.

I chose beautiful plates that were decorated around their rims and center with bright green leaves on brown twigs. The bowls were adorned with lovely orange stripes midway down the outside and on their bases. The goblets were so pretty; they had a red stripe that encircled the goblet's cup and another at the base of the goblet's stem. I thought all this brightness and newness would be just the thing for our upper room.

After I made my choices, it was now time to pay the potter's wife. Haggling began again. First the wife announced, "Twelve silver coins".

I said, "Ten!"

Then she said, "Nine". And so it went until she finally said, "I know your Mother, and I know she is a good woman, because she has been very kind to me." At that point, we settled for six silver coins, and shook hands to finalize the deal.

James thanked me and then packed all the plates, bowls, and goblets very carefully. I swiftly went home to help my mother complete her tasks. I felt a sense of accomplishment that I had been helpful to my mother.

Excitement built in our house with the day of preparation. We double-checked that we had all of the dishes ready, along with the leg of lamb and spices, as Passover would be tomorrow.

I placed the pot, now full of water, on the grill on top of the oven. Soon steam rose from the pot; then a few bubbles appeared, and finally, a rolling boil began in the pot. Father now lifted the boiling pot off the top of the oven and set it on the ground. There was a large stone near the oven. He picked it up and held it out over the boiling pot. Then he dropped it. "Plop!" It went into the pot, creating a wave of boiling water that splashed over the rim of the pot and flowed down all the sides of the pot. It left a trail of steam from the sides of the pot, and now the pot was thoroughly clean.

Father now began the process of cleaning the plates, bowls, and wine glasses. He took a plate, held it in the towel, and dipped it into the hot water. Then he rotated the plate and dipped the remaining part in the hot water. He repeated the process with each of the plates, dipping them and drying them. Once they were cleaned in the hot water and dried, he placed them in a large basket.

Next he took a bowl, held it in a towel and dipped it halfway into the hot water. He turned the bowl over again, and dipped it again in the hot water. He dried it and repeated the process until all the bowls were clean and stacked in the basket as well.

Then he took the wine glasses, holding each one by the stem, cleaning the stem first. He then dipped each goblet's bowl into the hot water, swirling the water around inside the bowl. After lifting the wine glass up, he now held it by the stem and once more dipped the base into the hot water, repeating this until all the wine glasses were cleaned.

Mother asked me to go to the grinder mill in order to grind some of the wheat into flour. I took a basket and filled it with wheat from a large storage jar, and then I took the basket over to the millstone, which consisted of two circular basalt stones. The bottom stone has grooves cut into it, and the grooves radiated outward to the edge of the stone. In the center of the stone was a good-sized stake. This stake was used to hold the upper stone in place. However, the hole in the center of the upper stone was larger and here the wheat grains were poured down into the lower stone. The upper stone also had a large handle on the outside area of the stone. This handle was used to turn the upper stone and to grind the wheat that had been put down the hole which was between the two stones.

I took a handful of wheat out of the basket and carefully poured it down the hole by the stake. Next, I took the handle of the upper stone and rotated it around, and around, and around. This process ground the wheat grains into a fine white powder, which drifted out of the lower stone and into a large basin to collect the powder from the mill. I repeated this over and over until the basin below the mill was filled with ground flour. I scooped the powder up and carefully put it into a large bowl. I carried it back to Mother where she covered it up so that it was ready to make unleavened bread tomorrow.

After the grains were separated from the stalk, they were placed into the hole at the grinder; it was necessary that the grinder was sturdy and functional. The bottom half was shaped like a cone, whereas the top was a movable hour-glass stone. The grain was poured through the top, and then when ground, was used for the basis of flour for bread.

Mother then asked me to grind some corn for the stew. This became cornmeal and was used to thicken the stew that she would be cooking tomorrow.

Father is busily preparing to roast the leg of lamb that he had purchased at the Sheep Gate. He took the leg of lamb and pierced it with a pomegranate stick and held it over the top of the oven. Slowly, we began to rotate the leg of lamb over and over, again and again. Soon the leg of lamb began to turn from a red piece of meat to one now brown in color. The meat became darker and darker. Juice from the roasting lamb began to fall into the oven.

Finally, Father declared that the leg of lamb was now done. He took the roasted lamb over to the preparation table and began to cut it into small, bite-sized pieces. He put these pieces into a large bowl so it could be cooked in the stew tomorrow.

All the necessary preparations for the Passover meal are completed, including the food, the dishes, and the room. It had been a long day, and now it was time for much needed sleep.

Morning came with a wake-up call from Mother. I rose and quickly dressed; then hurried up to the upper room to make sure that everything was ready for Passover.

When I entered the upper room, it was still very dark there. I had a feeling that something was not ready. I bent over the table and looked at everything that was on the table: plates, bowls, wine glasses. Then I knew what was missing. I went over to the cabinet and opened it. All the lamps were still in their places. I had not put them out on the table. One by one, I took a lamp, inspected it to make sure that it had oil and a good wick. Then I placed each lamp on the table. Soon I had placed all the lamps on the table and they were all ready to be lit just before the Passover meal would be served.

The lamps were very important because the Passover meal would begin late in the evening around five or six o'clock. I checked the hospitality table to make sure water was in the pitcher, a towel on the table, and scented oil was in the flask. Now all was ready for the Passover meal!

For the home to be bright at night time, clay lamps were used. The wicks would extend from the lamps spouts that would have soaked up the olive oil contents which was used as fuel.

As I left the upper room, I paused at the head of the stairs and looked out over the city and the beautiful mountains that surrounded Jerusalem. The mountains were beginning to blink with sparks of light from the campsites of people who had camped and were also beginning to prepare their Passover meals.

I looked down into the courtyard and saw that Father had a fire going in the oven and sparks were floating up from the top of the oven.

I went down into the courtyard. Mother had filled the new pot of water and was now adding the pieces of the roasted lamb, onions, cut-up potatoes, carrots, lentils, and celery to the pot. She now started to stir the pot and soon it began to bubble. It needed to have something added that would thicken the stew. She went over to the table and picked up the bowl of cornmeal that I had ground into a flour. She began to pour a little bit of it into the stew so it would begin to thicken. This would now be called sop. She stirred the sop and continued to add a little more cornmeal into the pot. Soon it was thick enough to satisfy her.

Mother dipped into the pot and scooped out a small portion of the sop. She gave it to Father to see if he approved of it so that it now could be served in the upper room. He nodded his approval that it was good and was ready to be served.

Mother called me over and gave me the sop to take to the upper room to fill the bowls. I carried the pot upstairs, set it down on the table and filled the bowls that were at every other place where the disciples would sit.

The sop's basic ingredient was primarily the roasted lamb bits. The prepared and cooked vegetables were then added to the mixture.

"In this manor your loins are to be girded, your sandals, and your staff in your hand." (Exodus 12:11-13 RSV) In the book of Exodus, Moses wrote; it is the Lord's Passover. For I will pass through the land of Egypt that night and I will smite all the first born in the land of Egypt, both man and beast; and on all the gods of Egypt. I will execute judgement; I am the Lord. The blood shall be a sign for you, upon the house where you are, and when I see the blood, I will Passover you and no plague shall fall upon you to destroy you when I smite the land of Egypt." (Exodus 12:11-13 RSV) This initiated the term Passover.

Moses also told the people that they were to be ready at a moment's notice to leave Egypt. He told them to keep their staffs ready and their sandals on their feet. Pharaoh was so angry that he told the people to get out and leave immediately. They left in such a hurry that they did not take anything to leaven their bread. Therefore, the unleavened bread became symbolic of their hasty departure from Egypt, as well as a symbol of the Passover.

Mother now took the flour that I had ground in the grinder. She added some water and a little salt to the flour and began to stir. Soon the flour turned into dough. She took a small piece of the dough and rolled it into a small ball, about the size of an egg. She then placed the ball into a large bowl, continuing to make small balls with the rest of the dough. She carried the bowl filled with the small balls of dough to the oven.

Father had placed a bronze cooking bowl upside down on the top of the grill. He sprinkled a little bit of oil on the bronze bowl.

Mother came over and took out one of the balls of dough; she began to flatten it out and soon she had a very flat piece of dough. She took this flat piece of dough and placed it on the inverted pan. She lifted the small piece of dough to see how it was cooking. When she saw that it was golden, she then turned the piece of dough over so that it would cook on both sides. She repeated this until all the balls of dough were flattened, cooked, and placed on a plate. She gave instructions to me on how these flat pieces of cooked dough balls were to be handled. She explained that this was now bread, and bread was a very sacred thing which had to be handled with both hands at the same time. She then instructed me to take this plate of bread to the upper room and set it down on the table. With both hands, I was to lift one piece off the plate and place it on the guests' plates.

It was the daily custom for the woman to bake bread for the family. Pictured are two different kinds of ovens that would have been used.

At Jesus' place there were four plates and on each of these four plates I placed a piece of bread, using both hands. I then went around the table from the inside and placed one piece of bread with both hands on each of the plates where the disciples would sit.

Mother was over near the table with a mortar and stone grinding tool. She was preparing to make haroseth. She was crushing the apples, walnuts, raisins, figs, apricots, dates, and then she added a small amount of honey and red sweet wine. The crushed results took on a dark, thick-like jam and was called mud by the Israelites. When the bowl was filled with this mud, she gave it to me and instructed me to, "Take this upstairs and place it in several bowls around the table." She also gave me several cinnamon sticks, saying, "Place several of these in the bowl of 'mud' when you put it on the table."

I recalled an early lesson from my father, who told me that the symbol of the "mud" was when the Pharaoh told the Israelites that they must make bricks for his building projects, but they were to use no straw. This made being a slave in Egypt, trying to make bricks without straw, a very hard job.

Mother arrived in the upper room, carrying a large bowl filled with bitter herbs, radishes, onions, horseradish, garlic, and other bitter tasting vegetables. She gave these to me, and I knew to divide these and place them in several bowls around the table.

Next, she handed me a bunch of parsley. She explained that I needed to fill four bowls with water, then go to the cabinet and take two lumps of salt and hold them over each bowl. I was to grind them together so that the grains of salt filled the bowl a little bit so that it would make saltwater. Then I was to place several sprigs of the parsley into each of these saltwater bowls.

I remembered that when people took a sprig out of the bowl, the few drops of saltwater that would drip was to remind everyone of the tears that were shed over the loss of loved ones when they crossed out of Egypt.

I went down into the courtyard, and Father was standing at the grill on the oven. He had placed several of the eggs on the top of the grill and was baking them. I asked him, "How do you know when the eggs are baked?" He smiled and then pointed to one of the eggs. Small brown dots began to appear on the egg. He said, "When the egg becomes totally covered with the brown spots, then the egg is done." Soon all the eggs were done and I took them up to the upper room and placed them in bowls around the table.

Father now entered the upper room carrying a large goatskin filled with sweet wine that he had bought at the wine shop. He began to fill the four wine glasses that were in front of each of the disciples. He filled the wine glasses only about a third of the way full. He then instructed me to follow him with a pitcher of water and to fill each wine glass that had wine in it with an equal amount of water as wine. The reason for this diluted wine was that the Rabbi would remind those present that they should not get drunk at Passover. The meaning for the four glasses of wine is explained in Exodus 6.

1. "I am the Lord and I will bring you out from under the burdens of the Egyptians." (Exodus 6:6 RSV)

2. "I will deliver you from their bondage." (Exodus 6:6 RSV)

3. "I will redeem you with an outstretched arm and with great acts of judgment." (Exodus 6:6 RSV)

4. "I will take you to be my people." (Exodus 6:6 RSV)

At the Passover meal, later in history later called the Seder, four wine glasses are placed at each participants place. Jesus speaks as each individual cup of wine is consumed. Each sentence gives Jesus' intentions for the one who drinks from the cup.

He speaks: "I am the vine, you are the branches. He who abides in me, and I in Him, he it is that bears much fruit. As the branch cannot bear fruit by itself, unless it abides in the vine, neither can you. I will deliver you from bondage, and I will redeem you." (John 15: 3-5 RSV) (Exodus 6:6 RSV)

"I will take you as my people, and I will be your God." (Exodus 6:7 RSV)

"You shall know that I am the Lord." (Exodus 6:6-7 RSV, John 15:1-10 RSV)

JESUS SERVES
PASSOVER MEAL

N ow, the Passover table was set with food, and the
lamps were lit.

Father, Mother and I were standing around the table,
admiring how beautiful the Passover meal looked and smelled.
Suddenly, the door of the upper room opened and in walked
Jesus! He stood tall and had very kind eyes that reflected His
divine soul.

He walked over to us and greeted us, "My Peace I give unto
you." (John 14:27 RSV) As he said this, he accompanied his
words with a gesture of the hand to his forehead, then to his
mouth, and finally to his heart. My parents replied, "And also
to you." They then made the same gestures with their hands to
their foreheads, to their mouth and to their heart.

Jesus then went over to the hospitality table and prepared to
wash his hands. He took the pitcher over to the special large

stone jar that held water and filled the pitcher up with water that was pure and ready for the ceremonial use of washing hands. Then he carried the pitcher back to the hospitality table. He held his hands with the fingertips pointed up. Now he poured a small amount of water that was equal to 1 ½ egg shells full. He then poured this water over his fingertips so that it would flow down into the basin. He did this with both hands. Then he made a fist of his hands and rubbed them together in his palm. This meant, at this stage, his hands were wet with water, but they remained unclean. Next, Jesus held his hands with his fingertips pointed down, and he poured the same amount of water over them, starting at the wrists. This water then ran off the fingertips into the basin, thus making both of his hands clean.

Now Jesus walked around the table. He picked up a baked egg and tapped the egg to see if it was truly baked. He continued his inspection of the table. He nodded here and there to his disciples and my mother who affirmed His approval of the specially completed setting of this Seder meal. When he was satisfied, he smiled at mother with a smile of appreciation for her delightful and meaningful preparation.

Father and Mother had prepared the food.

Mother then noted that her husband and John Mark were the ones who had set the table.

Jesus then walked over to me and smiled, seeming to validate my meaningful assistance with my mother.

I was so pleased by his attention that words did not come easily, but then I finally said, "I am honored to set the table for you."

With all the preparations completed, and now approved by Jesus, I couldn't help feeling little "pings" of excitement and anticipation.

The disciples were arriving, entering the upper room, and performing the ritual of washing their hands. Soon it was time for us to leave them to their Passover meal. Mother and Father made their way to the door of the upper room. Mother motioned to me to go down the stairs and prepare for sleep. This day had been a long day, preparing, cooking, and serving the Passover food.

I put on my blue striped nightshirt and sat on my bed. I wondered what Jesus would do during the Passover meal. Would he perform a miracle like the one at the pool of Siloam where he healed a blind man? Or, like the one at the wedding where he turned water into wine? Or, maybe something completely new?

My curiosity got the best of me. I decided to quietly sneak up the stairs and see what Jesus might do at this Passover meal.

I picked up a small stool from the corner of my room, and I then tiptoed up the stairs to the upper room. I didn't dare go inside the room, but I went around to the back of the room where there was a window. Here I put my stool down and sat down on it. I could see and hear what Jesus said and did in the upper room as they served the meal.

I did not know whether or not he would do something out of the ordinary while celebrating this Passover. I looked into the upper room and could see that all the disciples were lying down around the table. John was to the right of Jesus and Judas at Jesus' left.

[The following scriptures are related directly to the upper room on the night of Jesus' last Passover meal with his disciples.]

Jesus: "So Jesus sent Peter and John, saying, "Go and prepare the Passover for us, that we may eat it." (Luke 22:8 RSV) They wondered where will he have us prepare it? Jesus then said to them, "Behold, when you have entered the city, a man carrying a jar of water will meet you; follow him into the house which he enters, and tell the householder, "The Teacher says to you, where is the guest room, where I am to eat the Passover with my disciples?" And he will show you a large upper room furnished; there make ready." And they went, and found it as he had told them; and they prepared the Passover." (Luke 22:8-13 RSV)

Then the mother of the sons of Zeb'edee came up to him, with her sons, and kneeling before him she asked him for something. And he said to her, "What do you want?" She said to him, "Command that these two sons of mine may sit, one at your right hand and one at your left, in your kingdom." (Matthew 20:20-21 RSV)

John: One of his disciples, whom Jesus loved, was lying close to the breast of Jesus; (John 13:23 RSV)

Now about eight days after these sayings, he took with him Peter and John and James, and went up on the mountain to pray. (Luke 9:28 RSV)

And he took with him Peter and James and John and began to be greatly distressed and troubled. (Mark 14:33 RSV)

Judas: Jesus answered, "It is he to whom I shall give this morsel when I have dipped it." So when he had dipped the morsel, he gave it to Judas, the son of Simon Iscariot. (John 13:26 RSV)

He answered, "He who has dipped his hand in the dish with me, will betray me. (Matthew 26:23 RSV)

Peter: And he told his parable: "A man had a fig tree planted in his vineyard; and he came seeking fruit on it and found none. (Luke 13:6 RSV)

And someone said to him, "Lord, will those who are saved be few?" And he said to them, "Strive to enter by the narrow door; for many, I tell you, will seek to enter and will not be able. When once the householder has risen up and shut the door, you will begin to stand outside and to knock at the door, saying, 'Lord, open to us.' He will answer you, 'I do not know where you come from,' Then you will begin to say, "We ate and drank in your presence, and you taught in our streets." (Luke 13:23-26 RSV)

The Last Supper for Jesus to be with his disciples was served in a triclinium setting. A triclinium is a three-sided, U-shaped table, and each person, while eating, reclines on their left side and eats with their right hand. The left side of the table was for the most important persons present. In the first place was John, the Beloved. Second was Jesus, the Host, and third, on Jesus' left side was Judas Iscariot. Opposite on the right side, considered the least important persons, was Peter, who sat directly opposite John; he was to serve all the persons present. However, because of his seating, Jesus washed all of the disciples' feet.

Jesus looked around the table at all the disciples. He stood up and began to speak. As he did so, he picked up an unleavened piece of bread. He held it up with both hands, and then he raised it slowly up over his head brought it done signifying it came from Heaven. At that time Jesus took a small piece of the bread, ate it, signaling the end of the blessing, and then he returned the rest of the bread to the plate.

Next he took one of the four cups of wine that was in front of him. He held the first cup in both hands and raised it up over his head. He blessed the wine which came from the fruit of the vine. After he lowered the cup, he took a small sip of the wine as a way of concluding the blessing.

Now the disciples have had the food blessed and are now ready to eat. The bread serves as a spoon and fork; the disciples broke off a small piece of bread, folded it and picked up a radish with it. Then they dipped the bread into the haroseth and ate it.

The Passover meal moved into full swing, and the disciples ate and enjoyed the meal. Jesus knew that the last cushion on the far left of the triclinium was the servant's place. His job was to get up and wash the feet of all participants at the table. But,

Jesus sees that this was not being done. So he rose and went over to the hospitality table and removed his cloak (the outer robe), placing it on the hospitality table. He then took the towel from the hospitality table and placed it over his shoulder. Then he filled the basin of water from the pitcher. He went over to the first disciple, John, who was reclining at the table. Jesus knelt down, unlaced a sandal and gently removed it from John's foot. He gently lifted the foot, placed it in the basin, covered it with water, and bathed it, drying it gently with the towels.

A small table, referred to as a Hospitality table, is located just inside the door of the Upper Room. Those who entered had very unclean hands and feet. At the entrance would be a pitcher of water, a basin, and a towel. When all had arrived, Jesus removed His shirt, and with His gentle hands, he washed the disciples' feet.

One grimy foot after another, Jesus worked his way around the table. This was a servant's job, but none of the disciples had volunteered for the job, leaving it to Jesus. When he reached the last disciple, Jesus found him sitting on his feet.

Peter said to him, "Lord, do you wash my feet?" (John 13:6 RSV)

Jesus answered him, "What I am doing you do not know now, but afterword you will understand." (John 13:7 RSV)

Peter said to him, "You shall never wash my feet." (John 13:8 RSV)

Jesus answered him, If I do not wash you, you have no part in me." (John 13:8 RSV)

Simon Peter said to him, "Lord, my feet only, but also my hands and my head." (John 13:9 RSV)

Jesus answered him, "He who has bathed does not need to wash, except for his feet, but he is clean all over, and you are clean, but not everyone of you." (John 13:10 RSV)

Once Jesus finished washing their feet, he returned to the hospitality table and picked up his outer robe and put it on. He then went to his place at the table and said to them, Do you not know what I have done to you? You call me Teacher and Lord; and you are right to do so, for I am. The servant is not above his master, nor the one who sent him." (John 13:12-13 RSV)

As I watched Jesus perform this act of being a servant and now was seated, I could see that something was still bothering him. His head and eyes were down, but suddenly he straightened up, looked around at them, and said, "Truly, truly one of you is going to betray me!" (John 13:21 RSV)

The table exploded! Wine glasses tipped over, and the disciples threw their arms out wide exclaiming, "Tell us who it is of whom you speak?" (John 13:24 RSV)

Peter picked up a radish and tossed it across the table at John, who was leaning against Jesus. Cupping his hands around his mouth, he asked Jesus, "Lord, who is it?" (John 13:25 RSV)

I could not hear what John said, but Jesus nodded his head that he understood. Then Jesus spoke, "It is he to whom I shall give this morsel when I have dipped it." (John 13:26 RSV)

So he took a piece of bread and dipped it into the sop, gave it to Judas, Iscariot, and sang a hymn.

I watched the remaining eleven disciples follow Jesus go down the stairs, out into the courtyard, and off to the road that led to the Garden of Gethsemane.

As I sat there on my stool, I wondered what I had just seen there in the upper room. Jesus became a servant and challenged his disciples to be servants.

Then he pronounced a new covenant with the breaking of bread and the pouring out of the wine. Many years earlier, Moses was given, by God, a covenant made of laws on stone. Now Jesus was making a new covenant, a covenant that would be centered in the heart, and not written on the stones that appeared within the Temple of the Lord.

Sitting there on the roof outside the upper room, I heard the sound of marching feet very faintly coming from over the walls. There were bright, flaming torches winding down the roads from the Temple, and the closer they came, the noise increased. All of a sudden I could see that a crowd was coming up the road that led to our house. They came right up to the courtyard. The one who was leading them came in, went up the stairs, and opened the door to the upper room. When he saw that the room was empty, he turned around and ran down the stairs saying, "I know where Jesus has gone."

He then led the soldiers down the same road where Jesus and the disciples had just been. The soldiers were going to arrest

Jesus! What should I do? I'm only a young boy, and I'm only dressed in my nightshirt. Who will warn Jesus and the disciples?

I have to try to warn them. If I run, and take all the shortcuts, maybe I can beat the soldiers to where Jesus is so I can warn them of the soldiers coming.

I ran down the stairs and out into the street. I went down this road and that road until I finally reached the Garden of Gethsemane. The olive trees of Gethsemane were shrouded in darkness, and I had to grope my way along the walk. Where were the disciples? Suddenly, I saw them stretched out along the trail, sleeping. But where was Jesus?

Attempting to worn Jesus of the approaching soldiers on the path leading to the Garden of Gethsemane, a Roman soldier caught young John Mark, stripped him of his nightshirt, and then the young lad had to run back home naked.

["And a young man followed him, with nothing but a linen cloth about his body, and they seized him, but he left the linen cloth and ran away naked." (Mark 14:51-52)]

I went a little further on and then there was Jesus by a large rock, praying. You don't interrupt a person when they are praying, so I crept up on one of the sleeping disciples. I tapped him on the shoulder, but he just brushed my hand away. I tried another disciple and got no response.

"Please", I prayed, "someone wake up so you can warn Jesus that the soldiers are coming to arrest him!"

I was too late; suddenly the soldiers led by the disciple, Judas, burst in upon Jesus as he was praying. Then Judas rushed up and kissed Jesus. (This was a prearranged signal by Judas to identify Jesus from among the disciples.)

When this happened, there was a great deal of turmoil, pushing, and shoving by the soldiers and the disciples. But the disciples were no match for all the soldiers, and soon the disciples began to flee into the darkness.

All of a sudden, someone grabbed me and cried out, "Here's one of the disciples!"

When he grabbed me, I was so scared that I jumped straight up, twisted away, and fell to the ground, leaving my nightshirt dangling in the soldier's hands. I then turned and ran for my life. I did not mind that I had no clothes; all I wanted to do was to get back home safe and alive!

When I reached home, I went straight to my bed and pulled the covers up over my head. All I could think of was that I had failed to warn Jesus of His coming arrest. I had a hard time going to sleep. In fact, I even cried myself to sleep.

Morning came, and it was time to clean the upper room. My heart was heavy and my steps were slow as I dressed and went up to the upper room. When I opened the door and looked, I saw that the room was in a real mess. There was food spilled on the table, wine glasses tipped over, and the wine puddles on the table had dripped off onto the cushions.

I got our trash basket that had been filled with broken and chipped plates and wine glasses and I brought it over to the table, where I began to scrape the leftover food into it. I mopped up the wine with a towel and put it also into the basket. The cushions I took outside and hung them on the wall so that they would dry out. I straightened up the good wine glasses, bowls, and cups, and put them into another basket. Then I took both baskets down to the courtyard. Here I left the basket of good plates and wine glasses. There was a large bronze bowl on the oven, and it was beginning to get hot. The new dishes and plates would be washed in that hot water.

I carried the trash down to the garbage dump in the Valley of Gehenna. The fiery dump in Gehenna was a very inhospitable place. It smelled of badly rotten food, and there were burning fires; the smoldering smoke burned my eyes and my nose. I also had to be careful where I stepped, because there were broken glass plates, and I knew I could cut my feet if I weren't careful. I found a small place that seemed to be clean and clear of fire. Here is where I dumped the garbage.

I turned around and made my way out of the Valley of Gehenna. On my way home I stopped at the pool of Siloam and washed my face and eyes to get rid of the burning smoke.

When I reached home, I found my mother and father sitting in the courtyard. They looked very sad and shaken. Mother came over and put her arms around my neck. She spoke softly saying, "We have some bad news." She whispered to me "Jesus has been arrested by the Roman Guards."

"No", I cried, "he did nothing wrong! He only tried to help people. He didn't deserve that."

I wanted to be alone with my grief, so I went up to the roof where I had a place to be alone with my own thoughts and my pain. Here I tried to think things out. I had failed to warn Jesus about the soldiers who were coming to arrest him, and now he had been arrested. My heart was very heavy.

The next few days I lived in a fog. I didn't want to do my chores; I didn't even want to eat.

Now the Sabbath was here, and we all dressed to go to worship at the Temple. As we started out, the shofar sounded from the highest point on the wall of the Temple, calling us to worship. The sound of the shofar echoed over the city of Jerusalem, announcing the Temple was open for worship.

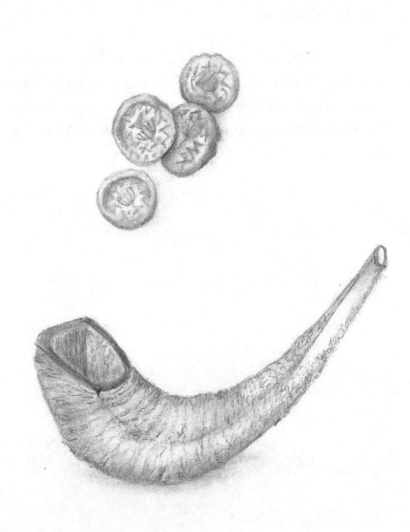

I walked with my father and mother the short distance to the Temple gates. Here there were bathhouses with mikvah baths. I entered one of the bathhouses and hung my clothes on the wall peg, and then I went down the steps into the pool where I submerged my body in the cool water. This was part of the ritual required in order to enter the Temple Mound.

After bathing, I dressed and went up the steps to meet my mother and father. We entered the Temple through the Huldah Gate. This took us under the royal store.

We climbed the stairs and entered the Temple enclosures and found ourselves in the Court of the Women. Right in front of us stood the Temple, which is the tallest building in Jerusalem. The door of the Temple is 30 feet tall. On either side of the door are two marble columns. Around these columns is a grape vine of pure gold. The leaves are also gold, and the grapes are larger than my head.

The Court of the Women is the largest court in the Temple area. At one end of the court, there are collection boxes. They are shaped like a trumpet. The mouth is wide and narrows at the bottom. Here we deposit our morning offering. The reason that they are wide at the top and small at the bottom is so that we cannot put our hand in and take money out of the collection box. Mother had just dropped a coin into one of the boxes.

All of a sudden, there was a loud cracking sound. I was standing and then I was thrown to the floor of the Temple Mount. The whole Temple Mount was shaking violently. People were lying in heaps and screaming in terror. I grabbed hold of the partition and pulled myself up. I held on to this railing in order not to be thrown down to the floor again. I looked out at the tall golden lamps in the courtyard there in front. They were swaying to and from, spilling oil from their very large cups.

The massive doors of the Temple were open and swinging back and forth. The priests who were inside the Temple tumbled, falling down the stairs and landing at the bottom in a heap. As they stood up they fled in terror, shouting. "At the same time the curtain of the temple was torn in two from top to bottom." (John 15:38 RSV)

The shaking of the Temple Mount was slowing down. We were able to get up and find our way through the crowds out of the Temple and back to our home. Here we found that there were minor damages to our home. The stone water jars in the courtyard had tipped over, spilling all of the water out. In the furnished upper room, I found the wine glasses had tipped over and rolled off the table, landing on the cushions. I quickly reset them on the table. Mother took a large jar from the storage room and made her way down to the Pool of Siloam where she filled the jar and brought it back home to refill the stone jars in the courtyard.

It was that afternoon that the disciple Peter showed up at our home. He stopped at the gate of our courtyard, and he looked both ways up and down the street to see if anyone had followed him to our home. He came straight to Mother and began to make arrangements for the disciples to meet again in the upper room.

After Peter had made these arrangements, I asked him, "Will you come and sit with me in the courtyard to tell me what happened in the Garden of Gethsemane and about the events that followed?"

I hesitated, but then I said, "I followed all of you disciples and Jesus, trying to warn you that the soldiers from the Temple were coming to arrest you, but I was too late. The soldiers burst in and arrested Jesus and I fled, running all the way home." I looked at my hands, too embarrassed to look directly into Peter's eyes.

Peter laughed when he heard me say what I had done, but then he countered with thinking it was I. He didn't know who it was, but he had seen a young person there in the melee. "So, it was you! I didn't know who it was, but I saw a young person there in the melee."

Peter had tried to fight off the troops, but I knew that I was outnumbered, so I went and hid behind a large rock. He paused, but I listened expectantly.

Peter explained that the disciple who had betrayed Jesus was Judas. Jesus passed by and he had his hands tied. Judas was leading them down the path back towards the Temple.

Then Peter also explained that he had followed behind the soldiers and Jesus, and how they crossed the bridge in order enter the Palace of Caiaphas. Jesus was then led into Caiaphas' Palace. I discreetly entered the courtyard of the Palace and sat down next to a fire burning there. I had not been seated very long when a servant girl came up and accused me of being a disciple of Jesus. I told her I was not and that I did not know him.

There was a man who came and accused me also of being one of the disciples, whom he saw in the garden. I answered him in the negative.

Suddenly, there was loud shouting from inside Caiaphas' Palace. Joseph of Arimathea told me what happened and what caused the outburst in the room.

When Jesus was brought into Caiaphas' hall, most of the Sanhedrin were gathered there to hear testimony against Jesus. The witnesses who testified were weak in their testimonies.

Then Caiaphas stood up and took over. He walked up to Jesus. I could see the anger on Caiaphas' face. The reason for that anger was because earlier Jesus had destroyed the tables of the money changers in the Temple and had taken a whip to the changers. As a result, Caiaphas had lost a great deal of money that those persons provided him. Now Caiaphas wanted to punish Jesus for his loss of income. Caiaphas stood in front of Jesus, pointed his finger in Jesus' face, and demanded, "Are you the Christ, the son of the Blessed?" (Mark 14:61 RSV)

Every one in the hall leaned forward to listen for Jesus answer. Quietly Jesus spoke saying "I am." (Mark 14:62 RSV)

And the High Priest tore his garments and said, "Why do we still need witnesses?" (Mark 14:63)"You have heard his blasphemy. What is your decision? And they all condemned him as deserving death." (Mark 14: :64" RSV)

Throughout the hall the Sanhedrin began to chant the accusation of blasphemy; it became louder and louder. The roar was heard from inside the hall.

Just then another person approached me, accusing me of being a disciple of Jesus.

I, Peter, grabbed the man, shouting, "I do not know the man." (Matthew 26:72 RSV)

As I was speaking, the door of the hall opened and Jesus came out. Jesus had heard what I had said. Jesus said not a word to me; he just looked at me. The look on Jesus' face pierced my heart.

Just then a rooster crowed a chilling call in the distance. I then remembered what Jesus had said, "I tell you Peter, the cock will not crow this day, until you three times deny that you know me." (Luke 22:34 RSV)

I fled from the courtyard and leaned against an olive tree. I broke down and cried bitter tears. When I gained control of my emotions, I followed the crowd as they went to Pilate's palace.

Only Pilate could pass a death sentence at that time, since he was the ruling leader representing Rome in Jerusalem.

The courtyard of Pilate's palace had a raised platform called the Judgment Seat from which Pilate held court. The members of the Sanhedrin began to present their case for a death sentence.

There were several witnesses who presented their claims. One of them said that Jesus had caused trouble up in the Galilee.

When Pilate heard that Jesus was from Galilee, he rose from his chair and asked the group below, "Is the Christ to come from Galilee?" The crowd agreed loudly! (John 7:41-42 RSV)

Pilate told them to take Jesus to Herod's palace, since Herod would consider the matter to be a local matter in Galilee.

The crowd then left Pilate's palace and proceeded on to Herod's residence. I followed at a discreet distance.

Herod wanted to see Jesus. All he wanted was for Jesus to perform some sort of miracle for his personal amusement. When Jesus was actually asked to perform a miracle, Jesus remained silent and did nothing.

Herod grew irritated and dismissed Jesus and the crowd, telling them to return to Pilate's palace.

When the crowd arrived back at Pilate's palace, Pilate proposed a plan to the crowd. By voice vote, one prisoner would be released by the crowd's choice, as was the custom at the time of Passover. Pilate told the centurion to bring two prisoners out and that he would let the crowd decide which one would be released.

At a given signal, the crowd would begin to shout out which one was to be released. The crowd had been stirred up by the priests and they began to scream very loudly for Barabbas, who was a murderer and a thief.

I tried to cry out, "Jesus", but I was silenced. Then Pilate released Barabbas.

Pilate now decided it was time to punish Jesus by scourging Him. This was a very harsh Roman practice.

A centurion now led Jesus into an inner courtyard. There they tied Jesus' face toward the pole, and stripped him of his robe. Next to Jesus at his back were two Roman soldiers, one on either side of him. Each had a flagellant whip. This instrument was about twelve inches long and had three leather straps. At the end of each of these leather straps, was a metal ball. Also on the straps were ragged fragments of bone and shells.

Beginning with the count of one, they began to strike Jesus back. This was a whipping, and it would inflict the victim with extreme pain. It was a very effective instrument for causing pain and bleeding. The Old Testament prophet, Isaiah declared, 'He was wounded for our transgressions; He was bruised for our iniquities.' (Isaiah 53:5 RSV)

I had to brush away my tears, and I had a lump in my throat. We could hear the crack of the whip and the horrible screams when Jesus was struck. I could not stand to hear the screams of Jesus, so I covered my ears and tried to block out the sounds of the whipping.

The soldiers finally finished their job of striking Jesus. When the count of 39 had been reached, they cut Jesus down. He fell to the ground. One of the soldiers picked Him up, and they dressed him in a purple robe. One of the soldiers thrust a long stick into his hand. Then a third soldier continued the mocking of Jesus by placing a crown of thorns on His head, pressing this thorny crown down over Jesus' face. The blood began to trickle down his face. He truly looked like a Suffering Servant, as was spoken of in Isaiah. "Surely He has borne our griefs and carried our sorrows, yet we esteem him stricken, smitten by God, and afflicted, ⁵but He was wounded for our transgressions, he was bruised for our iniquities; upon him was the chastisement that made us whole, and with His stripes, we are healed.' (Isaiah 53: 4-5 RSV)

This means of torture would render a victim a mass of blood and torn tissues. The first strokes of this means of torture would bruise the skin, causing the skin to blacken and turn blue. As other blows were continued, the skin would be shredded. The reason for this form of punishment was that Pilate hoped it would satisfy Caiaphas who had brought charges against Jesus.

In Isaiah, we find the following words, "Though your sins are like scarlet, they shall be white as snow, though they are red like crimson, they shall become like wool." (Isaiah 1:18 RSV)

Pilate then had Jesus brought into the courtyard in front of the large crowd that was gathered there.

(Peter looked at me to see if I wanted him to continue. I was spellbound and I nodded, "Yes.")

Peter continued with saying that Jesus was in great agony; each move caused him great pain. It showed on his face. What I had said made me sick to my stomach. Soldiers had beaten Jesus to a pulp, and He was on the verge of collapse.

At this point, Pilate stepped forward. With a sweeping motion of his arm, Pilate spoke to the crowd saying, 'Behold your King'. (John 19:14 RSV)

The chief Priests shouted back, 'We have no king but Caesar! Caesar is our king.' (John 19:15 RSV)

Pilate then asked the crowd, "Shall I crucify your King?" (John 19:15 RSV)

The crowd shouted back, "Crucify Him! Crucify Him!" (Luke 23:21 RSV)

Pilate washed his hands, drying them as he spoke to the crowd. "I find this man innocent. His blood shall be upon your hands." (Matthew 27:24 RSV)

A centurion nodded and two soldiers then brought out a crossbeam. This crossbeam weighed over 75 pounds. They placed it on Jesus' neck and used His arms to hold it in place. Pilate gave a signal, and with a wave of his sword, the centurion, along with other soldiers, led Jesus away to be crucified.

The road from Pilate's house, through the Hill of the Skull, is only a short distance, approximately 650 yards.

I, Peter, followed Jesus and I could see, as it was obvious, that Jesus was very weak from the beating, but also because he had not eaten much for several days. Every step that Jesus took, I could see that Jesus was having trouble walking and carrying the crossbeam. Jesus was walking and stumbling along the road. He fell and could not get up.

I wanted to help Him, but I was held back by one of the soldiers who pointed his sword at my chest. The centurion went over to the crowd that was standing by the road and selected a man named Simon the Cyrene from North Africa, to pick up and carry the crossbeam. Jesus staggered along behind the man carrying the crossbeam. When we reached the Place of the Skull, also known as Golgotha, Simon threw the crossbeam to the ground and walked away.

It was then that the soldiers pushed Jesus down onto the crossbeam where they stretched out his arms. One of the soldiers held one arm of Jesus and placed it on the crossbeam. Another soldier knelt beside Jesus and took out a nail from his bag. The nail was about six or seven inches long, and it was triangular-shaped. He placed the huge nail at the wrist of Jesus. The large, heavy hammer struck the nail's head, driving it through Jesus' wrist and into the crossbeam. Jesus' face grimaced in pain, and he cried out. The soldier then went around to the other arm and placed it against the wood. Then the other soldier took out another large nail and placed it above Jesus' other wrist, striking it and driving it through Jesus' wrist and into the crossbeam.

(As I, John Mark, tried to block out the very thought of anguished cries of pain from Jesus, and I felt the pain of the nails in my own hands. I reached out and touched Peter; we both were fighting back tears.)

Peter told me how the soldiers lifted the crossbeam with one soldier on each side of the beam, then they placed the beam up on top of the upright stake which had a notch where they could better secure it at the top.

Once this was done, a soldier then lifted Jesus' legs up and placed them one over the other with his feet flat against the upright beam. The soldier held them there, while the second soldier, with the nails and hammer, came and drove the nail through both of Jesus' feet and on into the stake.

(At this point, John Mark closed his eyes and covered his ears. He almost ran to the garden to throw up, but then he forced himself to continue to listen to Peter.)

Peter continued saying he could not bear to see or hear Jesus scream in agony. There were many people who had come to watch the crucifixion. Some were priests from the Temple; they jeered at Jesus and told him to come down from the cross. There also were many others, like the mother of Jesus who stood by weeping silently along with Mary Magdalene and the disciples, John, and James. We also stood there in shock.

I stopped and looked up at the sky. It seemed to be getting dark. It was about the third hour of the watch, when darkness covered the land. Because it was getting darker, the crowd moved closer to Jesus on the cross. All at once, someone in the crowd pointed up at Jesus, saying, 'he is speaking.'

I also moved closer so I could hear what Jesus might be saying. Jesus struggled but he said the following words, "Father, forgive them, for they know not what they do." (Luke 23:34 RSV) These were the words to those who had crucified him. There were words to the two thieves who were also crucified with him.

Jesus said to one of the thieves, "Today, you will be with me in Paradise." (Luke 23:43 RSV)

Jesus then looked at Mary, who was his mother and who stood nearby the cross with the wife of Cleophas, and Mary from Magdala. Now Jesus spoke to Mary, his mother, "Woman, behold your son." (John 19:26 RSV) Then he said to the disciple whom he loved, "Behold your mother." (John 19:27 RSV) John nodded and then took Mary to live in his own home.

The pain Jesus felt, was long and excruciating. Jesus cried out in a loud voice, "My God, why hast thou forsaken me?" (Matthew 27:41 RSV) It was a cry of desperation. The next words came, "I thirst." (John 19:28 RSV)

I could hardly hear Him, even though I stood right behind the centurion. We were both looking up into the face of Jesus. Jesus' eyes were glowing like fire as he looked at the people below Him from the cross. Then Jesus threw back his head against the cross, looked up to heaven and spoke, "It is finished." (John 19:30 RSV) With that, he took his last breath and died. At that very moment when Jesus died, an earthquake shook below their feet.

When this happened, people were falling down and picking themselves up. When I stood up and the centurion stood up, I heard the centurion exclaim, "Surely, he was the Son of God!" (Mark 15:39 RSV)

I was shocked to hear these words from the centurion. I went up to the centurion and asked him, 'Why did you say that?'

The centurion replied, I have seen many die by crucifixion, but this one was different. He did not die for a lie.

Now I, John Mark, felt I had to speak. "I know about the earthquake. I was at the Temple praying with my family when it happened. We also were thrown to the ground by the earthquake."

The centurions then removed Jesus from the cross, as ordered. They reversed the process of crucifixion, using a ladder and working as a team to bring Jesus down, who was still attached to the crossbeam from the stake. They lifted the crossbeam up out of the upright stake, which had been secured. Then they lowered it down to the ground. They worked hard to remove the nails from His body that was still nailed to the crossbeam. The nails would be used again for another crucifixion.

As they finished their work, two men stepped forward and presented an order from Pilate, giving them permission to take Jesus and place His body in a new nearby tomb. Joseph of Arimathea and Nicodemus were secret followers of Jesus; they also had witnessed the crucifixion.

These two men took Jesus' body, wrapped it in a white linen cloth, and carried him off the hill to place Him in the new tomb that had never been used for burial. They temporarily anointed Jesus' body with oil. Then they wrapped the body in a linen cloth after placing a small linen cloth loosely covering Jesus' face. When they had finished all this, they went outside the tomb and labored to roll the flat, heavy, round tombstone down the grooves that covered the entrance to the tomb. Inch by inch the stone slowly moved until it covered the tomb door.

As the sun was now beginning to sink behind the hill, John, both Marys and I watched all of this work of closing the tomb until it was complete. Then we all slowly and sadly walked away, each returning to his or her own home.

Peter finished telling me this story, and then he bid me goodbye, leaving by way of the courtyard gate.

The other ten disciples came one more time to the upper room, and this time they stopped at the gate to our courtyard, looking both ways down the road by my house. They wanted to be sure that no one was following them. They hurried up the stairs and entered the upper room. When they were all inside the room, I locked the door. They were like sheep with no shepherd. They were deeply depressed and the fear showed on their faces.

Peter then stood up and spoke, I don't know what you all are going to do. I have a business in Galilee; "I'm going back to go fishing." (John 21:3 RSV)

Then Peter, James and John stood up. They left the upper room, and I relocked the door. I could see that the rest of the disciples were still deep in thought as if in shock. I also was in shock and my mouth was completely open.

Suddenly, Jesus appeared in their midst and he began to speak carefully, fearing the disciples might think they were seeing a ghost. "Peace be with you." He said. (John 20:26 RSV)

Then Jesus spoke again; "Why are you troubled? And why do questionings rise in you? See my hands and view my feet and my wrists. It is I myself. Handel me and see, for a spirit does not have flesh and blood and bones as you see that I have." (Luke 24:38-39 RSV)

Jesus let the disciples approach Him to touch Him. They moved from fear to joy as they realized that He was alive and had risen from the dead. Jesus spoke, "Children, have you any fish?" (John 21:5 RSV)

It was then that I, John Mark, hurried to the cabinets and took out a plate on which Mother had fixed some cooked fish and a honeycomb. I brought the plate over to Jesus. He took the plate and smiled. When He took the plate of food, I was very cautious as I reached my hand out and put my finger into Jesus' wrist where the nail had pierced His wrist. I knew that Jesus was alive and real, for I had touched a living hand. This was a moment that changed my life, and I am sure it will change everybody's life when they realize that Jesus is the risen Lord.

A week later, Jesus appeared a second time in the Upper Room. I also was present at that time, as Mother had asked me to give the room a final cleaning. I was just leaving when the disciples arrived for a meeting. Peter nodded that it was okay for me to stay. Thomas had not been at the meeting when Jesus first appeared.

The door was locked again and Jesus appeared in the midst of the disciples. He spoke, saying, "Peace be unto you." (John 20:19 RSV)

He then turned and went straight up to Thomas and spoke to him, saying, "Put your finger here, and see my hands, and put out your hand and place it in my side; do not be faithless but believing." (John 21:26 RSV)

Thomas fell on his knees, looked up to Jesus, saying, "My Lord and my God!" (John 21:28 RSV)

I knew how Thomas felt when he touched Jesus' hands, for, I too, had touched Jesus and felt the same way that Thomas did.

There were other times that Jesus appeared to two different groups. He appeared to two disciples on the road to Emmaus. Jesus told the disciples, that he wanted to appoint them as ambassadors to go from Jerusalem to all the world and tell the people what happened here in the furnished Upper Room. He would give them power that will help them in that matter. Thus, it is written that the Christ should suffer and on the third day should rise from the dead; and repentance in His name and forgiveness of sins should be preached in his name to all nations beginning from Jerusalem." (Luke 24:46-47 RSV)

After Jesus was crucified, buried and resurrected, the people began to reflect and remember the many miracles Jesus performed while He was in Jerusalem.

One of those miracles that Mother heard was when she went to the Pool of Siloam. She had gone there to fill our water jugs from home, and there were always lively conversations going on with the women who were present.

She was told that Jesus was walking along. He saw a man who had been blind since birth and His disciples asked him, "Master, who sinned? This man? His parents? Why was he born blind?" (John 9:19 RSV)

"No one has sinned; he was born blind so that God's power might be displayed in the curing of Him who sent me while the daylight lasts," countered Jesus. (John 9:3 RSV) As Jesus spoke these words, He spat on the ground and then he made a paste from the spittle and soil there. Next He placed the mud mixture on the blind man's eyes and said to him, "Go now and wash in the Pool of Siloam." (John 9:7 RSV)

The man went and joined the line that was already waiting to go down the steps into the pool. When the blind man arrived at the water, he first splashed it on his face, and then again. He stood up and cried out, "I see men!" (Mark 8:24 RSV)

Mother said he frightened her with his loud screams. When the blind man approached my mother, he looked into her face with great joy and told her she was beautiful, and he then ran away, continuing to scream about his healing.

Mother returned home from the Pool about dinner time and was extremely excited. She began to tell me the story of this blind man's recovery of his sight. And when Father returned shortly thereafter, he also was told this wonderful story.

Meantime, the Pharisees were meeting to discuss this recent healing event. They began to question the man's parents. "Is this your son?" (John 9:11 RSV) My father was there and moved closer so as to better hear what was being said. About that time, one of the Pharisees spoke to the man who had gained his sight. "What did the man you speak of do to you?" (John 9:15 RSV)

The man's response was, "He put mud on my eyes and then instructed me to go wash in the Pool of Siloam. I followed those instructions, and I was immediately able to see." (John 9:15 RSV)

The Pharisees continued with, "How were your eyes opened?" (John 9:17 RSV)

The reply was, "The man called Jesus made a paste, smeared it on my eyes, and then I was told to wash in the Pool." (John 19:15 RSV)

The Pharisees then asked, "Where is He?" (John 9:12 RSV)

Answering in a strong voice, the response was, "I do not know." (John 9:12 RSV)

Father heard one of these men say, "This man is not from God, for he does not keep the Sabbath!" (John 9:16 RSV)

Another man asked the cured man, "What do you have to say about him since he has opened your eyes?"

Thereafter, the cured man responded, "He is a prophet." (John 9:17 RSV)

With disbelief, the Pharisees, hearing that, continued to question the parents of the cured man. Again they asked, "Is this your son, who you say is born blind?" (John 9:19 RSV)

The parents answered, "We know that he is our son, and that he was born blind." (John 9:20 RSV)

Being repetitive, the men who were "judging" the situation asked, "But how he now sees, we do not know." (John 9:21 RSV)

Again the parents spoke, "We do not know; ask him. He is of age; he will speak for himself." (John 9:21 RSV)

The parents gave these answers because they were afraid of the Jews, for the Jewish authorities had already agreed that anyone who acknowledged Jesus as the Messiah should be banned from the synagogue.

The Pharisees then called the young man who had been born blind and asked him again, "What did He do to you? How did he open your eyes?"

(John 9:26 RSV)

It was then that the Pharisees began to be abusive, saying, "You are his disciple, but we are disciples of Moses. We know that God has spoken to Moses, but as for this man, we do not know where he has come from." (John 9:29 RSV)

The young man spoke again. "Why this is a marvel. You do not know where He has come from, and yet he opened my eyes!" (John 9:30 RSV)

Argumentatively, the dialogue continued. "We know that God does not listen to sinners. But if anyone is a worshiper of God and does his will, God listens to him." Nobody has ever heard of the opening of the eyes of a man born blind." (John 9:31 RSV)

Another of the "judges" spoke, "If this man were not of God, he could do nothing."

(John 9:33 RSV)

Suddenly, the Pharisees gathered around one another and began to discuss what actions should be taken. The resulting decision was that the young man should be expelled from the synagogue.

As I sat in our courtyard, I could not believe that they could actually expel someone from the synagogue, so I spoke with my parents. "Can you really expel someone from the synagogue just because you disagree with the leadership of the synagogue?"

Mother explained, "There is more to what has happened to the young man."

Mother continued to tell me that when she was about to leave the Pool, a close friend arrived late to fill her pot. She, too, was quite excited, and quickly and enthusiastically repeated what had once happened to a young man at the temple steps.

When the young man was dismissed from the synagogue, he went straight to the steps of the Temple where the blind man had previously begged.

Jesus had heard that the young man had been expelled, and then Jesus immediately went looking for him. He found him at the Temple, and walking up to him, he noticed the sadness on the young man's face.

The young man pointed up to the Temple and said, The Pharisees questioned me as to how I received my sight and I said to them, "he put clay on my eyes and I washed and now I see." (John 9:15 RSV)

After hearing this, some of the Pharisees said, "This man who did this was not a man of God," (John 9:16 RSV) and then they asked me my opinion of you, who had opened my eyes. My reply to them was, "He is a prophet." (John 9:19 RSV)

Jesus continued with another question, "Do you believe in the Son of Man?" (John 9:35 RSV)

The young man with his newly found sight asked, "And who is he sir, that I may believe him." (John 9:36 RSV)

Then, looking directly into the man's eyes, Jesus spoke; "You have seen Him, and it is He who speaks to you!" (John 9:37 RSV)

The man's face lit up, and he cried out with great joy, "Lord, I believe and he worshiped Him. (John 9:38 RSV)

I, John Mark, know how I felt when I placed my fingers in the nail holes in Jesus body after the crucifixion. The young man could now see more than just a man with the name of Jesus, he had witnessed the Christ, the Messiah, the Son of God standing right in front of him.

With these many experiences I have had, especially this last one, I promised to share that knowledge with all who will hear the Word, for I, John Mark, will write this story in the first line of the gospel.

It wasn't long before Mother learned that Peter had returned from his fishing trip. He came to Jerusalem, and he was preaching daily in the Temple. She joyously shared about Peter with me, and I decided to go and hear Peter in the Temple. When I arrived at the Temple, there was quite a crowd gathered in the Courtyard of the Women. Peter and John were standing on the platform, facing the crowd and preaching the lessons Jesus had taught us.

Peter spoke with passion and a voice filled with emotion about Jesus' resurrection from the dead.

This Jesus was dead, but now is alive. Many were witnesses to this event.

Peter went on to say to them, "Repent. And he will allow every one of you to be baptized in the name of Jesus Christ for the forgiveness of your sins." (Acts 2:38 RSV)

I was amazed at how Peter spoke with such passion and such power. When he had finished speaking, I sought him out and asked him where he got the strength and the power to speak like this?

Peter beckoned me to come with him. Peter and I went out of the Temple and on to the steps that led up to the Temple. Here we sat down and Peter told me that after Jesus died, the disciples would come to the Upper Room to discuss what they were going to do. Jesus declined to stay with the other disciples.

He told them he was going back to the Sea of Galilee, as he had a fishing business there and was going fishing.

All of those who fish on the Sea of Galilee have favorite spots where they fish. Mine was a spot very close to shore called, Heptapegon, also known as the Place of the Seven Springs. The fresh water there comes from these springs and is a few degrees warmer than the Sea of Galilee, so the fish tend to gather there. The shape of the Sea of Galilee is like unto a harp, and is about 600 feet below sea level. Because the Seven Springs are warmer than the Sea, and it causes the temperature of the water to rise to about 72 degrees. This change in the water temperature tends to create a mist in the morning along the shore where it enters the sea.

Our boats were equipped with torches on their bows and we leaned over the bow of the ship as it glided over the sea. We looked for the fish as they were drawn toward the light. We fished all night and had not caught anything. Dawn was beginning to break over the mountains high above the sea, but it was still dark out on the sea. The mist was beginning to form along the shore and, suddenly, a figure in in the morning mist called out to us on the boat, "Children, have you any fish?" (John 21:5 RSV)

John, who was standing in the front of the boat answered, "No." (John 21:5 RSV)

As the mist began to rise, John could see a figure of a man. Suddenly, he thought that Jesus might be standing there on the shore, but he was not quite sure.

Then the figure that was now being seen better in the mist spoke. "Cast the net on the right side of the boat; and you will find some." (John 21:6 RSV)

We did as he said, and suddenly our nets were full of fish. Peter spoke and said, 'Peter, it is the Lord." (John 21:7)

Then I turned, put on my cloak, as I had been stripped for fishing, and I swam to the shore. When I arrived at the shore, I saw something that I thought I would never see. There on that small stretch of beach, my eyes beheld the Lord, as He was standing by a fire.

This scene was etched in my mind; I would never forget it. He had set charcoal in a fire that was burning; he was cooking fish and bread. I did not really want to ask Him who He was because I was afraid He might not be real. Now the other disciples pulled the boat to the shore and stood near me. They also were afraid to ask who He was.

Jesus now spoke, "Bring some fish that you have just caught." (John 21:10 RSV) I went back aboard the boat and brought a few more fish. I handed them to Jesus, and He began to cook them. I noticed His wrists were pierced by the nails.

Jesus then turned and said, "Come and have breakfast." (John 21:12 RSV)

We all gathered around the fire as Jesus served us. When we finished eating, Jesus beckoned me to come and follow Him. We walked away from the other disciples.

It was then that Jesus turned and spoke to me saying, 'Simon, son of John, do you love me more than these?' (John 21:15 RSV)

I answered him saying, 'Yes, Lord, you know that I love you.' (John 21:15 RSV)

Jesus then said, 'Feed my lambs.' (John 21:15 RSV)

A second time Jesus asked me, 'Simon, son of John, do you love me?' (John 21:16 RSV)

I was deeply hurt and said unto Him, 'Yes, Lord, you know that I love you.' (John 21:16 RSV)

Jesus' response was, 'Tend to my sheep.' (John 21:16 RSV)

A third time Jesus said to me, 'Simon, son of Jonah, do you love me?' (John 21:17 RSV)

Again I answered, 'You know that I love you!' (John 21:17 RSV)

Jesus said, 'Feed my sheep." (John 21:17 RSV)

Peter told me what Jesus had done was to give him the responsibility to become the shepherd of The Church.

Several weeks later, at Pentecost, Jesus gave the remaining disciples the power of the Holy Spirit to do His work.

When Peter had finished telling me what happened to him that day on the Sea of Galilee, he invited me to go with him to meet some people who had been baptized and who were now following the teachings of Jesus.

We walked to a house not far from my own house, and we entered the courtyard. I was amazed at how we were greeted! I was welcomed as a friend. I soon discovered several things about those who were now following the teachings of Jesus, the same ones Peter was teaching.

These followers were a group of people who practiced the art of being a friend to all people. They were people who prayed together and shared what they had with those who were in need. They were a happy group of people who showed what Jesus meant to them.

I liked them from the very first time that I met them. They were sharing what they had, and I also wanted to share about Jesus. I did not have land to sell as some of them, or goods, but I had something that had changed my life, so I shared with them what had happened to me there in that Upper Room after Jesus was crucified.

I, John Mark, told them how the disciples had also returned to the Upper Room because they were discouraged and were like sheep without a shepherd. They sat around the table and spoke in low tones about what had happened.

I continued my story by telling them how Jesus had suddenly appeared to the disciples, that He spoke to them, and showed them His hands and His feet. The disciples had difficulty believing it was true.

Then I told them that Jesus asked, "Have you anything to eat here?" (John 21:5 RSV)

Since I was the servant in charge of the Upper Room, I went to the cabinet and I took out a plate of fish and bread that Mother had prepared. I gave it to Jesus and He took it and ate it before them.

I, too, cautiously was able to put my finger into His wrist where the nail had pierced his hand, and it was then that I really discovered that He was flesh and blood; He was alive and had risen from the dead.

In that moment my life was changed. He was alive, and I believed!

When I shared this with the people in the courtyard, they, too, were filled with great joy at my witness. I told the story to other small groups there in Jerusalem as well.

One day after having told my story of the risen Lord, Peter asked me if I would go with him as he left Jerusalem and traveled around to other towns, preaching about the resurrected Lord. I excitedly accepted.

Peter and I traveled up and down the roads in the lands of the Bible. We stopped here and there, and Peter preached about

Jesus and what He had said. I kept a journal of all that Peter said about Jesus.

We moved on to town after town. At last we reached Rome. It was in Rome where the "People of the Way", as the early Christians were known, were being persecuted. Peter immediately began to preach about Jesus, the Christ, the Messiah. The messages and his delivery were powerful and meaningful. However, Rome and the Roman government disliked what Peter was saying.

The Roman soldiers set out to arrest and crucify Peter. Peter was crucified upside down because Peter said he was not worthy to be crucified in the same way as Jesus.

Earlier, Peter had asked me to write an accounting of "the Good News" about the life and teaching of Jesus. I had all of what Peter had said about Jesus in my journal, along with my own personal experiences. Peter requested that I document in writing everything from my journal. Today, I sit in a small room to begin fulfilling Peter's request.

I am getting ready to dip my quill into the ink so that I may document Jesus' life and teachings, as well as Peter's teachings.

I begin to write the first lines of a new gospel:

This is the beginning of the story of how Jesus Christ, the Son of God, brought the Good News for all mankind to hear.

BRIEF COMMENTS

"While teaching archaeology in Jerusalem, I had the privilege of teaching many pastors who came to study in the Holy Land. With great fondness I recall the conscientiousness of Bill Caldwell, who returned many years to continue his studies. Seeing how the Jewish roots of Christianity and studying the land contributed to the Bible coming alive for his congregation, he gave his life to help bring many pastors to Israel and its neighboring countries. Perhaps most encouraging to me has been to see the way he has continued his studies through his retirement, including his and his wife Julie's efforts to write and bring to publication this book."

Dr. James Fleming: Archaeologist, Biblical Scholar, Director of Biblical Resources, LLC in La Grange, GA

"Being of Jewish heritage, I have often thought about the harmony of Judaism and Christianity. After traveling in the

Holy Land of Israel with my father-in-law, Bill Caldwell, and my listening to his stories with reflections from the Old and New Testaments, such as this one herein, I have come to accept the connection. My heritage remains with me, and my current life as a Christian both fill my spiritual walk in a most meaningful way."

Gerard E. Cohen

"My husband, Charles, and I accompanied Rev. Caldwell on a trip to Israel and Egypt in 1983. I can say without hesitation that because of his enthusiasm for biblical archeology and love of the Bible, the Scriptures came alive for us. May this book do the same for others."

Katie Woodbury